SATURN AND THEIR RINGS

SATURN AND THEIR RINGS

Nymeria Publishing LLC

First published in the United States of America by
Nymeria Publishing LLC, 2021

Copyright © 2021 by S. N. Benenhaley

All rights reserved. Except as permitted under the U.S. Copyright Act of 1976, no part of this publication may be reproduced, distributed, or transmitted in any form or by any means, or stored in a database or retrieval system, without the prior written permission of the publisher.

Nymeria Publishing
PO Box 85981
Lexington, SC 29073
Visit our website at www.nymeriapublishing.com

ISBN 978-1-7363027-4-3

Printed in U.S.A

To Taylor Morgan Spires,
Such an innocent soul taken from this world too soon because the words of others and mental illness touched your life. You said I was destined for great things, and here I am.

I love and miss you, Morgan.

They say that Pluto is a lonely planet,

What was once a part of our planetary system, yet now just a mere dwarf entity,

Anxiously waiting in the background to be noticed once more.

However, I believe Saturn to be a lonely planet

It stands in the mighty shadow of its sibling, Jupiter.

It is in second place to it constantly, despite being so very complex and fascinating by itself.

It is known for its seven ring system, but not many know that its density is less than that of water, so it theoretically could float in a bathtub large enough to hold it.

It has the most moons of all the planets, 82 *and counting* as the years fly by us, with only 53 being named.

It houses Titan, the only moon that has an atmosphere, making it a possibility for life.

It has several powerful storms that ravage its atmosphere, such as the legendary "Dragon storm" and the hexagon shaped hurricane at the north pole.

It even rains diamonds from the skies and has mesmerizing cloud bands that paint the planet,

just like Jupiter.

Out of all of the planets within our solar system,

Saturn has been the one that has fascinated me most since learning of its density in 4th grade,

So, here I am.

Saturn finally spoke up.

Please Don't Break My Rings

There are several layers that surround me, rings you may call them,
They surround my rocky core of a heart,
Protecting me from the outside dangers of this hell of a universe,
A wall of barriers that would take a catastrophic collision to get through.

You want in so desperately, but you have to realize this:

Please don't break my rings unless you plan on staying here,
They took me millions of years to build up,
And if they're gone,
What do I do then?

Hexagonal Hurricane

There is a storm within me that even I can't control.

A part of me just wants to end it all,
So, the others can feel awful for what they've done.

A part of me wants to take my car and leave this uninhabitable planet,
Start a new life, and never look back again.

A part of me wants to let it all out,
Scream, cry, break some things, and just let the emotions go.

I said there was a storm within me,
And it is one that may seem organized from the outside,
With its perfect hexagon outlines.

But on the inside,
It is utter chaos that pulls at my heartstrings,
A teeter totter of emotions,
That's never fully balanced,
Always back and forth.

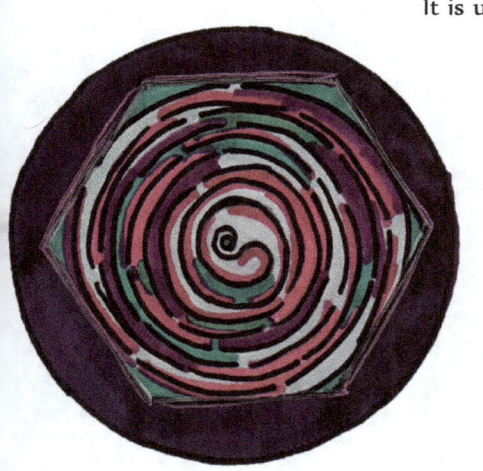

String of Pearls

There's a distinct break in the awful atmospheric depression shrouding my body,

And I can once again see the blinding lights of bright hope millions of miles away.

I shed thousands upon thousands of diamond tears, stinging my angry skin,

As I view the string of pearls, the brightness above the suffocating clouds.

I don't want to become so hopeful for this once in a lifetime chance,

But god it's so beautiful and finally I feel something again,

Not the suffocating clouds surrounding me, not the hard rock core at my center,

Not the superstorms raging through me, or even my many ring barriers.

I became so comfortable here with the planetary problems laid out around me,

That they weren't truly issues anymore; It was just something I was dealing with.

Just life.

I sulked in the suffocating clouds,

I suffered within my thick, ring barriers,

I permitted my core to harden into rock,

And I allowed the superstorms to swirl in me.

Maybe when the next break in the clouds come,

I can finally escape.

Saturn Has One of The Fastest Axis Spins

Dear God,

I can't stop spinning around in this fucked up galaxy of ours.

My eyes can't focus on the blurred images flashing before them.

The fast movement is consuming my thoughts.

I'm starting to think there's no point anymore in resisting it.

I can't stop spinning.

I can't stop spinning.

I

Can't

Stop

Spinning

New Moon

I thought I was the only one with issues, that saw the galaxy for what it truly was.

Everyone else around me just goes about their days,
following the same exact orbits,
Rotating throughout their tasks.

And then you came along.

Your eyes are parallel to mine,
You see the corruption, the flaws, and the pain.
But you still laugh and cry,
And let yourself be sad.

I'm grateful you entered my orbit right when you did,
 I can't imagine my systems of moons without you.

It's Better Off This Way

Why would I want anyone that close to me, like they were before?
I have the rocky ring barriers surrounding me for a reason,
And it isn't to attract others or anything of that nature.

You can't see the layers of my personality under the suffocating clouds,
Because I know that I am a lot to unpack and very few can handle that.

It's better off this way.

I don't want to feel the pain of a thousand heartbreaks,
Because I thought I was in love one time back in my day.

I really don't want to feel the pain again.
Just leave me be with my rings and all,

It's better off this way.

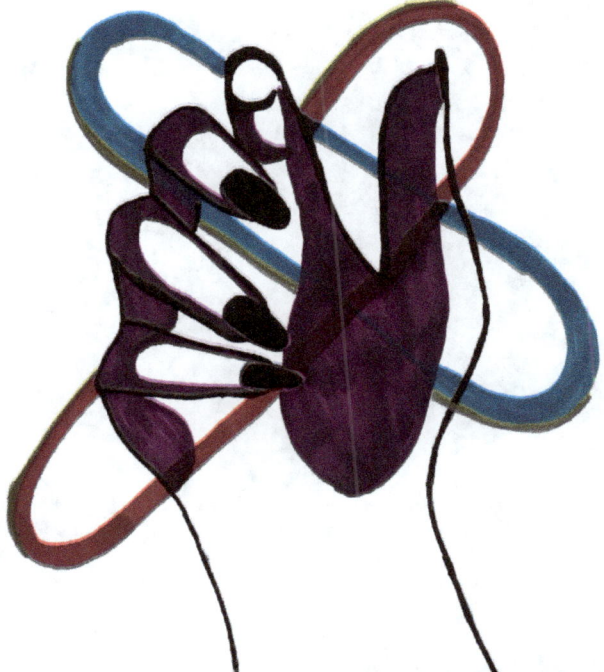

Retrograde

You may think I'm taking a step back,
Taking the time to tend to my tendrils,
And making space for myself in this orbit of mine.

But it's just an optical illusion.
It was always an illusion,
Nothing more.

You wouldn't have noticed if I hadn't told you.

"Dragon Storm"

This storm isn't a one-time phenomenon.

It rises within me and demands to be felt.

The coursing winds blow the tousled strands of my hair,

As the diamond rain shards tug at my scarred skin,

And the lightning lifts up the air around me.

It recedes back into the unknown depths of my planet,

But I can always feel it lingering,

Waiting to rise again in another couple of years.

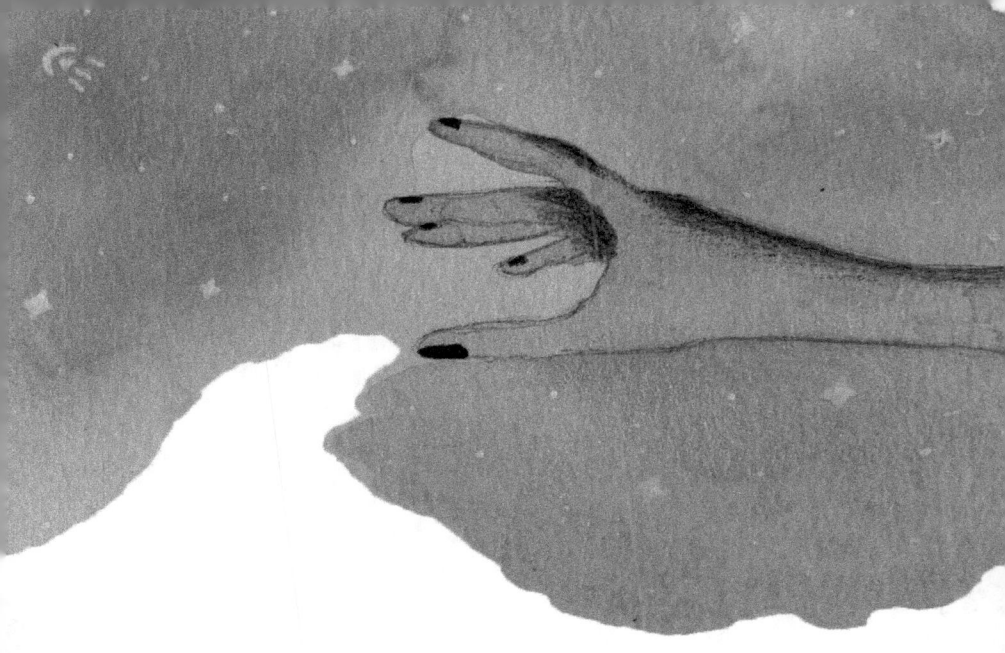

Gravity

Don't get too close and show me affection so soon,
Because my gravitational pull will bring you in,
And next thing I know I'll want you close to me in my orbit of important people.

You'll change your mind and try to escape,
Leaving a void there that I will have to wait to fill again,
Until the next individual comes around.

Do you know how long I waited for someone like you,
To come into my unappealing atmosphere?

Please don't leave me.

Paper Rings

Don't let my large rings fool you,

They are but paper thin and not completely whole.

There are cracks and crevices everywhere within them.

I am not this rock hard, heartless being,

That others may try to portray me as.

You will have to see for yourself.

Planetary Conjunction

Can't we just align with each other perfectly, just this once?
I'm tired of the separation and hard work we have before us
I know it won't be perfect all the time,
But please for the sake of the universe.
Just let us align.

I don't have the energy within me to fight anymore,
So please just try this once so we can make it work.
I promise it will be worth it once we get there.

Planetary Family

You would think within this family system,

I wouldn't feel so alone,

Yet here I am:

In a crowded galaxy,

Those circling around me,

The loneliness is my only friend.

Seven Year Seasons

I envy your drastic seasonal changes,

Your warm, flowery springs,

Blazing hot summers,

Comfortable autumns,

And snow-filled winters.

I may have seven year seasons,

But they are all in the same:

Frigid, bone chilling temperatures,

Raining diamonds and other crystalloids.

There isn't much difference between them,

And so, I'm stuck in the blandness of my planet.

At least the skies give me a view,

Of beautiful blue and violet hues,

Above the banded clouds of hydrogen and ammonia.

A Notch In The Ring

Every little notch in my rings from the intergalactic hits over the last thousand years can't take me entirely down, but in total there will be that last one that completely causes the fall.

The breakdown. The end.

A complete change. 360 turn.

That will absolutely break a ring or two,

Maybe even disrupt my gravity

Throw off my axis angle.

Destroy a couple of my moons in its path.

Would I still be Saturn without my rings and all?

Then I'll just have to build myself back up from the beginning,

And watch as the cycle unfolds again in another thousand years.

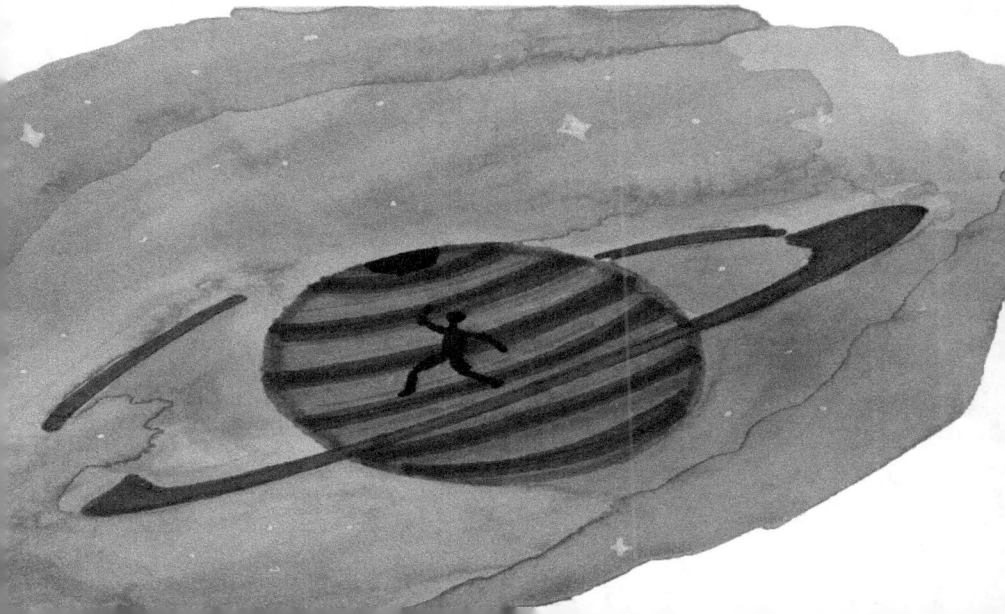

Metallic Oceans

You are lucky your oceans are merely just water molecules,

Because I am drowning in my own liquid metallic hydrogen oceans,

Desperately reaching for someone's hand or even a lifeboat,

To help within this raging storm at sea,

And yet no one will help me,

Because it's my planet.

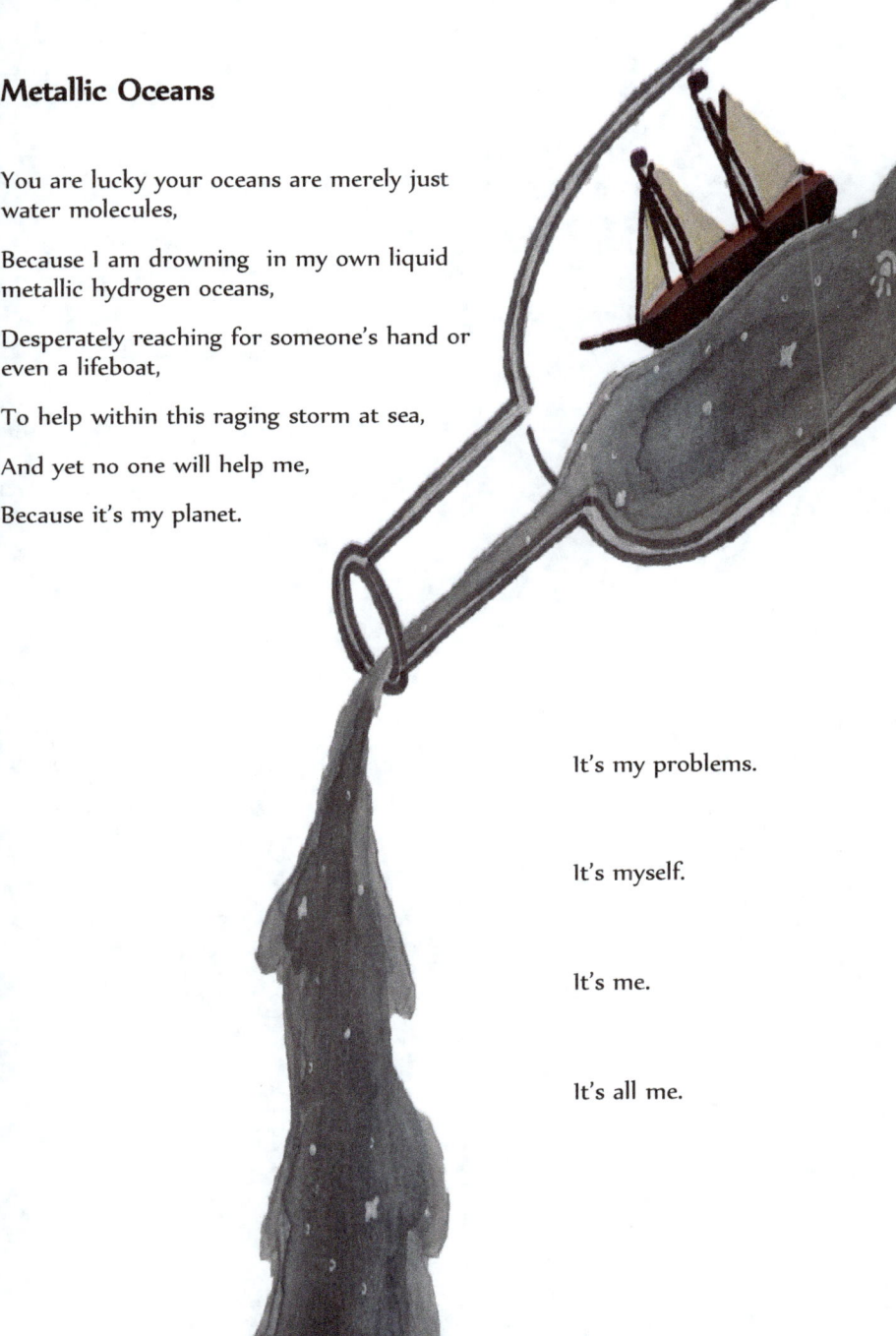

It's my problems.

It's myself.

It's me.

It's all me.

Many Moons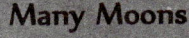

You said you loved me to the moon and back,

But I am Saturn.

I have 82 moons *and counting*

So, I told you that you must love me in many ways,

You couldn't though.

So, you moved onto someone much simpler,

With less moons and a lesser gravitational pull.

I was too big and mighty for you,

But that's okay.

Someone else will come around,

And discover my greatness again one day.

"The Ringed Planet"

I am more than just my dainty little rings that you coined this nickname after.

Admire my cloud bands, my superstorms, my moons, and all.

I am a whole entire planet, an entire intergalactic being.

I am not just my rings.

I am not just my rings.

Titan and Enceladus

I didn't know that you were just going to use me for my parts and pieces,
Several of my moons that orbit around me in a clear path.
I guess I'm not that interesting,
And once you got what you wanted,
You left me in the vacuum of our galaxy.

They were more interesting,
More intriguing than I ever will be,
So, I can't entirely blame you.

I am incapable of holding life and being understood completely like them,
So I guess it is okay.

Voyager 1

Why would you make the journey across the galaxy to catch a glimpse of me,
Explore my storms, worship me like the interesting entity that I am,

Just to leave me shortly after landing?

Were my voluptuous views pleasant?
Did you savor every second watching me?
Was I even worth an expedition?
Are you going to tell the others about my oddities, traits, and more?

Why is everyone like this?

I am not to just be stared at like art upon a wall
You must love and admire me too.

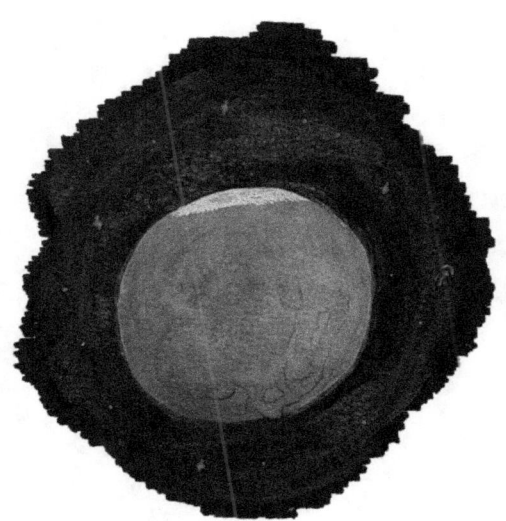

Ceres

You didn't learn about her in the textbooks,
Class lectures, or informational videos.

It is sad to say in the very least.

We have a whole other planet close by,
And I didn't know until by my own means.

You aren't alone, Ceres.
We are a fucked up family solar system.

This is all for you.

Cassini

I am not all layers of hard rock barriers and cold ice hearts,

There's room for love and passion in there somewhere,

You just have to explore me:

My thick, cloudy layers,

My deathly frigid temperatures,

And my millions of devastating storms.

I promise I am worth the expedition.

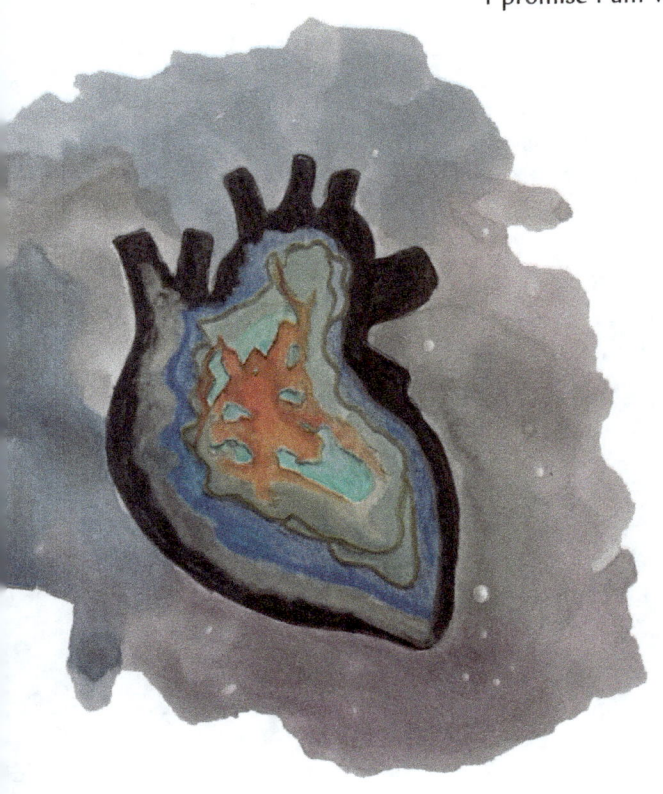

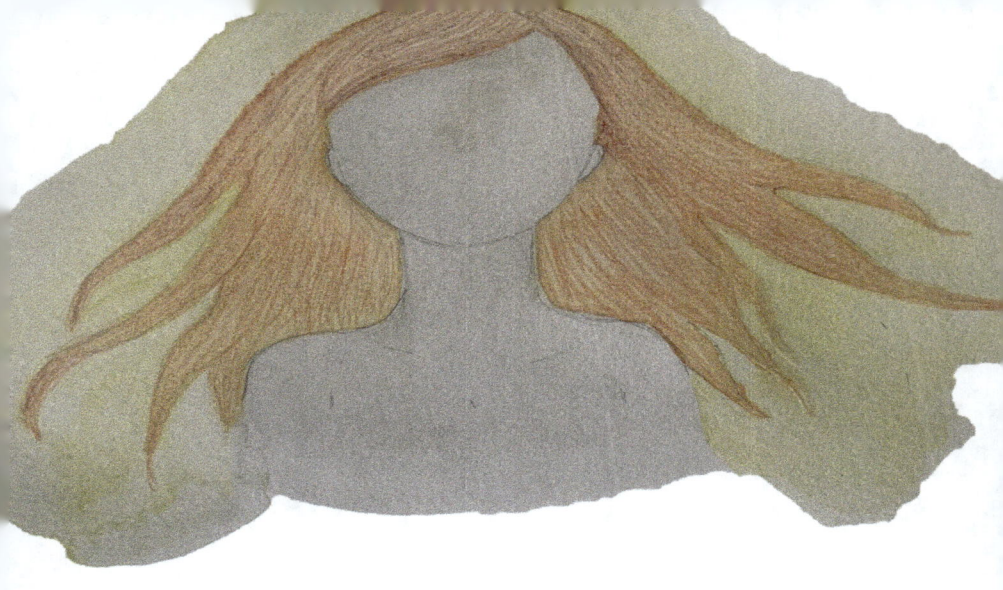

Heliocentric

The universe revolves around her,

So of course, you wouldn't notice me,

And the others close by.

That's okay, though.

We orbit, revolve,

And watch as you give her the attention.

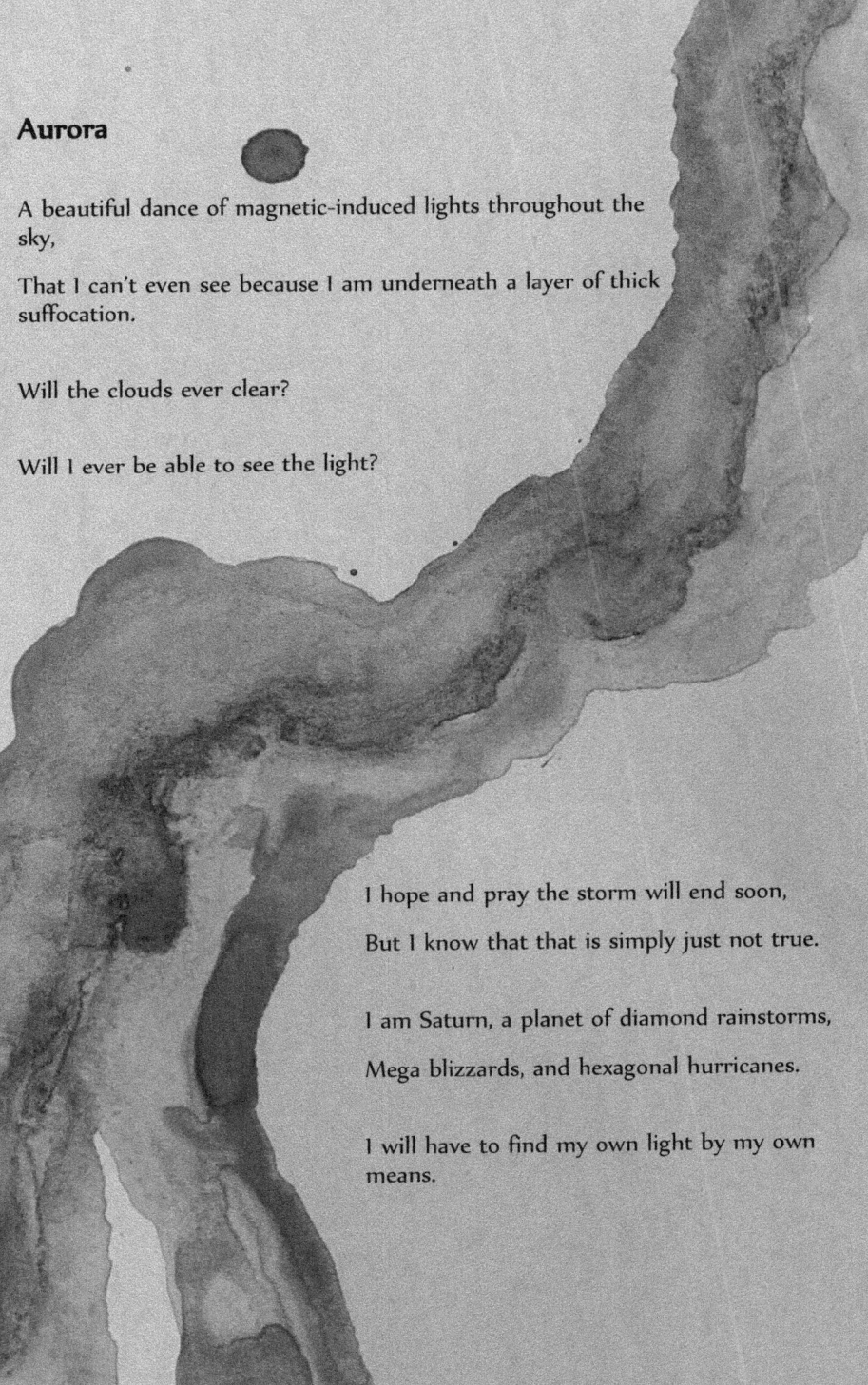

Aurora

A beautiful dance of magnetic-induced lights throughout the sky,

That I can't even see because I am underneath a layer of thick suffocation.

Will the clouds ever clear?

Will I ever be able to see the light?

I hope and pray the storm will end soon,
But I know that that is simply just not true.

I am Saturn, a planet of diamond rainstorms,
Mega blizzards, and hexagonal hurricanes.

I will have to find my own light by my own means.

Solar Flare

I beg for the deadly heat to come my way,
Just so I can feel something again.

I want to be encased in its flames,
Just so the cold freeze of space isn't my only friend.

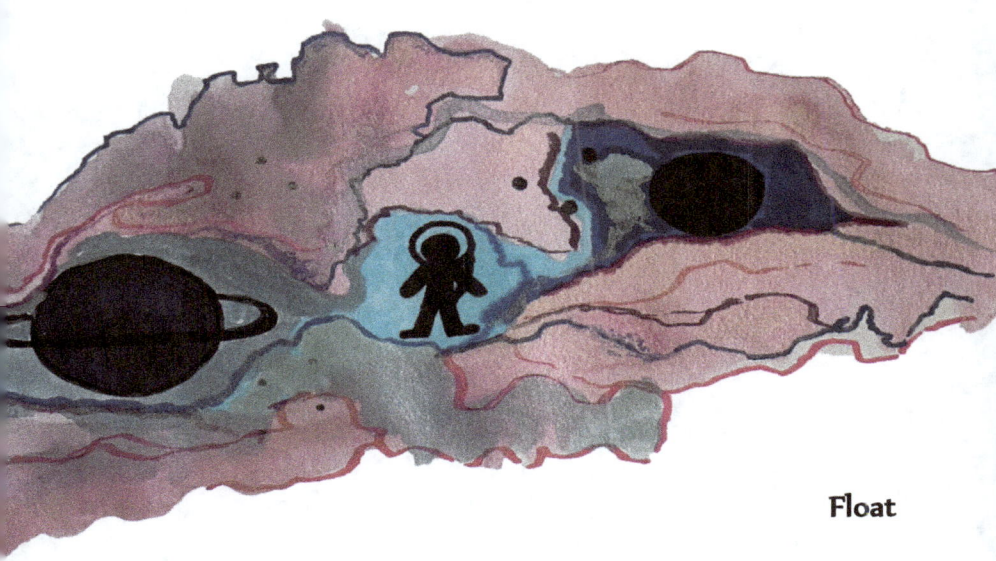

Float

There are many moments where I can see myself from the outside,
Floating above my body, my planet,
Seeing the cloud bands unravel,
Superstorms surging,
Rings existing,
Moons orbiting,
And the other planets going about their days,
As if nothing is going on,
As if they don't see me,
Just floating.
Watching my own self from above and beyond.
This isn't normal,
Yet they don't bat their eyelashes,
As I seem to just float,
And not truly exist in this universe,
That allows me to live like this.

Milky Way

This galaxy is filled with so many things that I do not quite understand and that is perfectly okay.

We shouldn't understand absolutely everything going on in our lives.

This world, this galaxy is so very complex.

It wouldn't be fun if there wasn't some sense of mystery and magic around us,

A sense of wonder and curiosity closing in on us in a bubble,

And making us question the depths of our oceans,

The number of galaxies present,

And the smallest particles that make up life and things as we know it.

Understand that you won't know everything about this galaxy,

And relish in the inquisitiveness of it all.

29 Year Orbit

You would think I would have plenty of time to have my life together with how long it takes for a full orbit to occur,

Yet here I am.

Floating through the universe without any true plans.
I'm just trying to navigate through without hitting anything,
Desperately trying to stay on my narrow orbit,
And not cross into other's boundaries.

How can I plan when I don't know what exactly is around me?

The universe isn't this organized set of plans and neither am I.
Stars explode, planet's cores burn up, and black holes form.

I am done with your expectations that I should have my life together at a certain set point in time.
My destinations are not mapped out before me like your dainty little constellations,
I will have to navigate as I go through and just conquer what I can as I go throughout the galaxy.

Acknowledgements

First, I have to start by thanking my family for the unconditional support of my educational path, passions, and hobbies. You all have always known that I was capable of great things and harnessed such an environment to allow me to spread my wings.

Second, I want to thank all of Taylor Morgan Spires' family for supporting me in all my endeavors. We came together during the tragic loss of our Morgan and I am thankful to still have the connection to you all over these last 6 years.

Third, I want to thank all of my teachers and professors that encouraged me to submit my writing to contests, sign up for English honors, and take those extra writing classes in college. You saw the raw talent and helped me harness it into a strength, for which I am now extremely grateful for.

Lastly, I want to extend my thanks to all of my friends that have stayed by my side all these years. You were the first round of individuals to reread my scripts, poems, and stories for the classes and contests. Your help was and still is greatly appreciated.

www.ingramcontent.com/pod-product-compliance
Lightning Source LLC
Chambersburg PA
CBHW062201100526
44589CB00014B/1904